New York Knicks

Michael E. Goodman

CREATIVE EDUCATION

Published by Creative Education
123 South Broad Street, Mankato, Minnesota 56001
Creative Education is an imprint of The Creative Company

Designed by Rita Marshall

Photos by: Allsport Photography, Associated Press/Wide World Photos,
Focus on Sports, NBA Photos, UPI/Corbis-Bettmann, and SportsChrome.

Photo page 1: Walt Frazier
Photo title page: John Wallace

Library of Congress Cataloging-in-Publication Data

Goodman, Michael E.
New York Knicks / Michael E. Goodman.
p. cm. — (NBA today)
Summary: Describes the background and history of the New York
Knickerbockers pro basketball team.
ISBN 0-88682-884-8

1. New York Knickerbockers (Basketball team)—History—Juvenile litera-
ture. [1. New York Knickerbockers (Basketball team)—History.
2. Basketball—History.] I. Title. II. Series: NBA today (Mankato, Minn.)

GV885.52.N4G66 1997   96-51064
796.323'64'097471—dc21

First edition

5 4 3 2 1

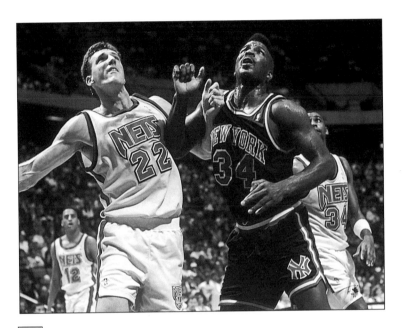

The short-story writer O. Henry called New York "the wonderful, cruel, enchanting, fatal, great city." O. Henry understood that New York is a mixture of many things—some of them wonderful and some of them harsh and frightening. New York is truly a melting pot. People of all different nationalities and ethnic backgrounds live together there. Some of the richest people in America live in New York, and some of the poorest, too.

Above all, New York is famous as the artistic capital of the United States. Great theaters line Broadway, and hundreds of smaller theaters are found throughout the city. The country's

Power forward Charles Oakley.

John "Bud" Palmer averaged 9.5 points per game, leading the Knicks their first season.

largest museums are located in New York, as are such great concert halls as Lincoln Center, Carnegie Hall, and Radio City Music Hall. The bustle and excitement of New York carries over into the sports world, too. Through the years, millions of fans have been captivated by the exploits of football's Jets and Giants, baseball's Mets and Yankees, and hockey's Islanders and Rangers. Yet on the streets and playgrounds of this great city, the sport that has always seemed to stand out above the rest is basketball. And one pro sports team has both thrilled and broken the hearts of more New Yorkers throughout the years than any other—the New York Knicks.

Since the Knickerbocker franchise was established in 1946, more than 300 players have donned the New York team's orange and blue colors. Such former greats as Carl Braun, Dick McGuire, Nat "Sweetwater" Clifton, Willis Reed, Bill Bradley, Dave DeBusschere, Earl "The Pearl" Monroe, and Walt Frazier helped shape professional basketball. Today, such stars as Patrick Ewing, John Starks, Larry Johnson, and Charles Oakley are carrying on the proud Knicks tradition. The team has an exciting history that includes more than 30 playoff-caliber seasons, seven appearances in the championship series, and two world titles.

AN NBA ORIGINAL

In 1946, the Knickerbockers became a charter member of the Basketball Association of America (BAA). Three years later, the Knicks and several other teams from the BAA merged with a few squads from the National Basketball

Knicks great Earl "The Pearl" Monroe.

League (NBL), which was failing on its own, and formed the National Basketball Association (NBA).

Right from the start, the Knicks established themselves as one of the classiest teams in both the BAA and then the NBA. The Madison Square Garden Corporation, which owned both the club and the arena in which it played, put a very special man in charge of the team. His name was Ned Irish. As the founding father of the Knicks, Irish had a clear-cut philosophy: "We will create first-class conditions for a first-class team in a first-class city," he declared.

Thanks to Irish, the Knicks boasted the league's first training camp, the first athletic trainer, and the most aggressive scouting program in the nation. Irish himself coached the team during its first year. Then he convinced Joe Lapchick, one of the finest college coaches in the country, to leave nearby St. John's University and take over as coach of the Knicks in 1947.

"I went after Lapchick because he knows how to win, because he loves the game, because he cares about his players, and because he's a first-class New Yorker through and through," Irish said.

Lapchick's college reputation also helped draw top young athletes to the Knicks. In 1947, for example, Carl Braun—an outstanding baseball and basketball prospect—decided to break his contract with the New York Yankees just for the chance to play basketball under Lapchick. Braun quickly became the offensive leader of the Knicks and was named to the league All-Star team five times during his 12-year career in New York.

1 9 4 8

Rookie Carl Braun pumped in 47 points against Providence—a team record that stood for 12 years.

8

Braun was soon joined in New York by Harry Gallatin, Vince Boryla, Dick McGuire, and Ernie "Doc" Vandeweghe (Kiki Vandeweghe's father). Together they became known as the "New York Five." They were small (no player was over 6-foot-6) but lightning quick, and they played great team basketball. New York's legions of basketball fans, who had often packed Madison Square Garden for college games, now began filling the arena for pro contests as well. Big-time professional basketball in New York was no longer a dream; it was a reality.

Guard Dick McGuire, one of the game's first great passers, led the NBA in assists with a 5.7 average.

The "New York Five" placed second to the Syracuse Nats in the NBA's Eastern Division during the 1949–50 season, and the following year roared through the playoffs all the way to the NBA championship series. The battle for the 1951 NBA title between the Knicks and the Rochester Royals was one of the most exciting ever. The championship wasn't decided until the last minute of the seventh game. The Knicks, down by 16 points in the first half, battled back to tie the score with less than two minutes remaining. But with only 40 seconds left, Rochester star Bob Davies hit two free throws to put the Royals ahead for good. Rochester went on to win the game and the championship, 79–75.

The Knicks weren't discouraged by the close loss. They became even stronger during the 1951–52 season, when Nat "Sweetwater" Clifton, Connie Simmons, and Max Zaslofsky joined Coach Lapchick's lineup. With their talent and depth, the Knicks were sure they would soon win an NBA title. And they came close. New York reached the league finals in 1952 and 1953, only to fall both times to the Minneapolis Lakers.

Willis Reed, big enough . . .

. . . and Bill Bradley, fast enough.

The Lakers were led by George Mikan, the best big man in the game. Mikan's size was the main difference between the two clubs.

Kenny Sears led the team in scoring for the first of two years in a row.

"The reason we didn't win the championship," Clifton explained, "was because we didn't have a center; I wasn't big enough and Harry [Gallatin] wasn't big enough. Connie [Simmons] was big enough and he could shoot, but he couldn't rebound and he wouldn't guard. So that was our downfall."

The Knicks stayed near the top of the league until 1956. Then age began to slow down some of the club's best players, while teams like Boston, Syracuse, and Philadelphia added younger and quicker stars. New York finished the 1955–56 season in a tie with the Syracuse Nats, each with a 35–37 record. The two teams staged a one-game tie breaker

Rebound leader Harry Gallatin.

to see which club would make the playoffs, and the youthful Nats quickly eliminated the Knicks.

The loss to Syracuse marked the beginning of a sad period in Knicks history. Starting with the 1956–57 season, New York finished last in its division nine out of 10 years and made the playoffs just once. Nothing New York management did could change the team's luck. Trades were made, and such talented new players as Kenny Sears, Richie Guerin, and Willie Naulls joined the squad. Although they were terrific individual players, they didn't make much of a difference in the team's record. The college draft didn't help either, as such first-round choices as Johnny Green, Darrall Imhoff, Paul Hogue, and Art Heyman—each an All-American in college—fizzled out in Madison Square Garden.

New York fans were desperate for a winner. The team leaders scoured the country in search of a coach who could reverse the club's losing trend. They finally found the man they needed sitting at a desk in their own front office. He was William "Red" Holzman, the team's likable, mild-mannered head scout.

Richie Guerin was the first Knick to break the 50-point barrier with a 57-point show against Syracuse.

HOLZMAN INSTILLS A TEAM CONCEPT

Red Holzman had two major qualities that helped him become a great coach. He had a good eye for talent as a result of his scouting experience, and he believed strongly that for a club to win, individuals had to be willing to sacrifice some of their own statistics for the good of the team.

During the 1960s, Holzman helped bring to New York a group of players who were ideally suited to his "team concept" style of play. Between 1964 and 1968, the Knicks drafted out of college such key players as Willis Reed, Bill Bradley, Cazzie Russell, Walt Frazier, and Phil Jackson.

One of the most important moves in Knicks history occurred in December 1968, when New York acquired power forward Dave DeBusschere from Detroit for starting center Walt Bellamy. The trade did two vital things for the Knicks. It allowed Willis Reed to move from forward to center, a position that better suited him. And it brought DeBusschere, one of the smartest and toughest players in NBA history, into the Knicks' lineup.

Now all the pieces were in place to form a smooth, winning machine. The various Knicks players were different from each other, but they fit together perfectly. First, there was Willis Reed, the team's captain and inspirational leader. At 6-foot-9, Reed was not as tall as many of the league's top centers, but he was wide and strong, and he had the heart to go up against—and overcome—bigger players. Joining him up front were DeBusschere, who was all power and determination, and Bradley, who didn't run or jump very well but who was a quick and deadly accurate shot from the outside.

The team's backcourt floor general was Walt Frazier, nicknamed "Clyde" because of the fancy suits he loved to wear off the court. He reminded people of the well-dressed gangster in the popular movie *Bonnie and Clyde*. At the other guard spot was Dick Barnett, an awkward-looking string bean who was outstanding on both offense and defense.

Coming off the bench were such fine role players as Cazzie Russell, who would put up shots from anywhere

1 9 6 9

In his first full season as coach, Red Holzman led the club to a 54–28 record—its seventh best ever.

Walt Frazier, the smoothest Knick of all.

within 40 feet of the basket and make them, and Phil Jackson, a long-armed defensive specialist who also had a good hook shot on offense.

Holzman molded these individuals into an outstanding unit. Each player knew his job and knew he could count on his teammates to support him on offense or defense.

"It was a chemistry with the Knicks, a blend of individuals that resulted in communication," said DeBusschere. "We knew each other's personalities well enough that we could all accept criticism. I could say something to Willis or Clyde. Clyde would really listen. He took it; he absorbed it. We found that when we got those lines of communication open, the willingness to sacrifice to help our team or teammates, not expecting anything in return, was a common goal. We went out to win; we were going to perform at our heights. That was fun, really fun."

1 9 6 9

Dave DeBusschere made 70 rebounds in the Knicks' four-game playoff series versus Baltimore.

COURAGEOUS VICTORY

The fun for New York fans reached its height during the 1969–70 season. Early in the year, the club won 18 consecutive games, an NBA record at the time. Even when the streak stopped, the Knicks found a way to keep winning. They finished the year with 60 victories, a club record unmatched until 1992-93. But it was the team's performance during the 1970 playoffs that is best remembered.

The Knicks battled past the Bullets in seven games and routed the Milwaukee Bucks in five contests to reach the championship round. There they faced the Los Angeles Lakers, who were led by Wilt Chamberlain, Jerry West, and Elgin Baylor. The clubs split the first four games, with two going into overtime. New York won game five, but it was a costly victory. Before halftime, Willis Reed drove down the lane for a layup, but tore a muscle in his right leg and crumpled to the floor in great pain. Dave DeBusschere cried out when he saw Reed go down, fearful that the team's hopes of winning the NBA title had collapsed as well. Somehow, the rest of the Knicks pulled together and won game five, but the situation looked bleak.

1 9 7 0

Willis Reed led the Knicks in scoring for the fourth season in row.

The Knicks' chances of winning their first NBA title seemed even slimmer two nights later, when, with Reed out of the lineup, Wilt Chamberlain dominated the Knicks inside and led the Lakers to a 22-point victory. It was clear that the Knicks needed Willis Reed desperately, but could the team captain play again?

Ninety minutes before the start of game seven, Reed went out on the court in empty Madison Square Garden to test his leg. It was sore, and he couldn't move very well to his right, but Reed decided to play anyway. He announced his decision to his teammates. "It was like getting your right arm sewed back on," said Cazzie Russell. As the New York fans and the media crowded into Madison Square Garden for the final game, they saw Reed limp onto the court for a few warm-up shots. As though the Knicks had already won the championship, a spontaneous roar erupted in the Garden.

The crowd's roar became almost deafening when Reed sank the first two baskets of the game for New York. There was no stopping the Knicks now. As it turned out, Reed scored only those first four points. But Frazier, Bradley, Barnett, and DeBusschere more than made up for the captain

Knicks versus Lakers, a battle to remember (pages 18–19).

Walt Frazier led his teammates in scoring and minutes played for the first of five seasons in a row.

on offense, while Reed did a good job of stopping Chamberlain on defense. By halftime, New York led 61–37 en route to a 113–99 triumph. But the final score is not what people recall about that night. The memory that lingers in the minds of Knicks fans is the sight of Willis Reed courageously limping onto the court before the cheering crowd.

REACHING THE TOP AGAIN

Holzman's Knicks kept up their fine play throughout the early 1970s. They reached the Eastern Conference finals following the 1970–71 season and went up against Los Angeles again in the NBA finals the next year. This time, however, the Lakers got their revenge, winning the series four games to one.

By 1972–73, the New York roster had changed a little. Earl "The Pearl" Monroe, one of the most creative scorers in NBA history, now started in the backcourt with Walt Frazier. The Pearl quickly adapted to Coach Holzman's team concept and showed he could play strong defense, too. The Frazier-Monroe backcourt duo became one of the best of all time.

At the end of the 1972–73 season, the revamped Knicks took on the Lakers for the NBA championship for the third time in four years. Los Angeles won the first game. Then New York came alive. With Frazier in the driver's seat and Reed controlling the boards, Coach Holzman's powerful machine rumbled over the Lakers for four straight wins. For the second time in four years, the Knicks stood alone at the top of the NBA.

As a tribute to the Knicks' championship stars, the jerseys

of Reed, Barnett, Bradley, DeBusschere, Frazier, and Monroe now hang from the rafters of Madison Square Garden.

Unfortunately for Knicks fans, their heroes began to age, and the club slowly slid in the NBA standings as teams in Boston and Philadelphia rose. Holzman stayed on as coach through 1976–77, gave up his job to Willis Reed for a season and a half, and then returned to lead New York for three more campaigns. The team made a strong comeback in 1980–81, winning 50 games. The stars then were center Bill Cartwright and guards Ray Williams and Micheal Ray Richardson. But the old magic was gone. The club fell to the division cellar the next year, and Holzman decided to retire.

1 9 7 2

In his first of three seasons with the Knicks, Jerry Lucas scored 1,282 points and made 1,011 rebounds.

A NEW "KING" IN NEW YORK

The 1982–83 season saw two new leaders in New York. Running the show was new head coach Hubie Brown. He was a very strict general, ordering his team to press and trap on defense and to run patterned plays on offense. It took nearly half the season for the Knicks players to adapt to Brown's coaching style. The club lost its first seven games and was 17–27 at the season's midpoint. Then the Knicks took off in the second half of the year, going 27–11 and earning a playoff spot.

One of the main reasons for the team's success was the arrival of Bernard King, a new offensive star. King, who grew up in Brooklyn, New York, had been a standout performer for the New Jersey Nets several years before. Then problems with drugs and alcohol almost ruined his career. Now he was ready for a comeback.

21

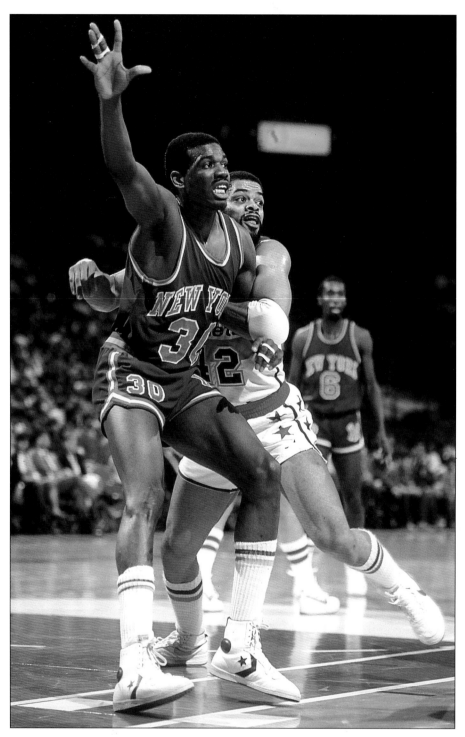

NBA All-Star Bernard King.

A fierce competitor, the 6-foot-7 King possessed the body of a forward and the speed and balance of a fleet-footed guard. He had excellent shooting range, but his specialty was the inside drive. "Bernard has an incredibly explosive first step to the basket," marveled Coach Brown. King also had the ability to get off his shot while on the way up, before a defender could block it. All of these weapons made him an offensive machine.

Micheal Ray Richardson led the team in assists (572), steals (213), and points (1,469).

King averaged more than 26 points per game to lead New York's attack in 1982–83. He topped that number with a league-leading 32.9 average the next year. During those two seasons, King and Hubie Brown pushed the Knicks to a level that surprised basketball experts. Explaining the team's success, a writer for the *Official NBA Guide* noted, "Coach Hubie Brown badgered his team to play above its talents by utilizing two not-so-well-kept secrets . . . defense and Bernard King."

Unfortunately, New York came to depend too much on King. Early in the 1984–85 season, King severely tore ligaments in his knee while making one of his patented drives to the basket. He didn't return to the lineup for nearly two seasons, and the team's promising future seemed to head to the hospital with the fallen star. The Knicks plunged in the standings, winning 23 fewer games than they had the previous season, finishing with a miserable 24–58 record.

Mark Jackson was named NBA Rookie of the Year, joining his fellow Knicks Willis Reed and Patrick Ewing.

The loss of Bernard King and the collapse of the Knicks did have one positive result for New York. The team finished so low in the standings that it gained the right to pick first in the 1985 draft. They chose the best big man in college—Patrick Ewing.

"The Patrick Ewing Era Has Begun," announced a May 13, 1985, headline in *The New York Times* sports section. Ewing had been one of the greatest defensive players in college history. He was Georgetown's all-time leading rebounder and shot-blocker. He was the second all-time Georgetown scorer. He was a team leader who took the Hoyas to the college Final Four three times, once resulting in a national championship. He was a member of the 1984 United States Olympic gold medal-winning basketball team. And those are just some of the many highlights of Ewing's college career.

Which of these accomplishments did Ewing consider to be his greatest college thrill? None of them. He was proudest of something that happened off the basketball court. "My most satisfying moment was the day I graduated and received my degree from Georgetown," Ewing said. "This was the fulfillment of my mother's dream. She worked so hard to make it possible for me to get a college education."

Ewing looked forward to many satisfying moments as the Knicks' center. And New York fans expected a lot from their new savior. But the road was rocky at first. Despite Ewing's dominating presence in the middle and the fine play of another rookie, guard Gerald Wilkins, the 1985–86 Knicks never played well together. The players' offensive creativity was stifled by Hubie Brown's strict system, and the young, inexperienced Knicks didn't play good team defense either. The result was another last-place finish in the Atlantic Division.

Over the next two years, the club made several key changes. Brown was fired, and his former assistant, Rick Pitino, took over. Pitino drafted point guard Mark Jackson out of St. John's and put him in charge of the team's offense. He also devised a pressing, suffocating defense that drove other teams crazy.

Jackson's ability to race up court and fire pinpoint passes opened up the New York offense and helped Patrick Ewing become one of the most feared scorers in the league. Ewing's scoring, combined with his uncanny talent at shot-blocking, made him a two-way threat.

The Knicks were on their way back, and crowds began to pour into Madison Square Garden again. Following the 1987–88 season, New York reached the playoffs for the first time in four years and began a string of postseason appearances that has continued into the 1990s.

Hitting 118 of 296 bombs, Trent Tucker made the three-point shot a key to the Knicks' attack.

NEW DECADE . . . HIGH HOPES

As the team moved toward the new decade, Knicks management refocused on the team concept, Red Holzman's secret of success. They knew it was not enough to have one of the best big men in the game; Ewing needed rebounding and scoring help if the team was going to make a strong rise in the league standings.

First, power forward Charles Oakley was obtained in a trade with Chicago, and his aggressive rebounding helped to

Patrick Ewing, dynamite on the court (pages 26–27).

Power forward Charles Oakley led the Knicks with 920 rebounds, averaging 12.1 per game.

relieve Ewing of some of the pressure under the boards. Next, sharpshooter Kiki Vandeweghe—whose father had played with the early Knicks—joined the club to provide outside scoring punch.

Before the 1991–92 season, the Knicks also added a new coach. The man chosen was Pat Riley, who had led the Lakers to four NBA championships during the 1980s before retiring to become a broadcaster. Riley decided to return to coaching to take over the Knicks. "There was really only one job I was interested in coming to, and that was New York," said Riley. "It's a town with a team, a media, a fan base, and a management equally hungry to win. For those reasons I knew it was the right time and place for me."

Riley did exactly what he was hired to do—he turned the Knicks back into a championship-caliber team. Ewing continued to dominate all aspects of the game, ranking among the NBA's top 10 in scoring, rebounding, and blocked shots, as the Knicks got as far as the conference semifinals, where they lost to defending NBA champs Chicago in a seven-game series.

Emerging as one of the Knicks' best players was John Starks. Starks, signed out of the Continental Basketball Association, was considered a "find." He proved to be a defensive specialist and a deadeye from three-point range. He began as the Knicks' sixth man, but played well enough to eventually earn a role as a starter.

"I made a lot of difference in a lot of fourth quarters," said Starks of his contribution. "I don't have that big of an ego. The main thing is winning."

Starks, Ewing, Oakley, and Riley managed 60 wins in their

second season together, and the Knicks played like a team that had found the right chemistry. Riley was voted Coach of the Year, and the Knicks played nasty defense. But the Bulls beat the Knicks in the conference finals once again.

Then, in the off-season, the Knicks' wildest fantasy came true: Michael Jordan, the Bulls' backbone, retired, and the Knicks believed it was finally their turn to go to the finals. Starks and Ewing had All-Star seasons, as did co-captain Oakley, who was seventh in the league in rebounding and was voted to the NBA All-Defensive first team.

Defensive master John Starks's 92 steals set the club's season record.

"I don't think there's any better defender in the league," Knicks assistant coach Jeff Van Gundy said of Oakley. "He's been the heart and soul of the team. Whenever he's on the floor, he brings our game up to a new level."

As expected, the Knicks dominated the Eastern Conference and roared through the playoffs. They made the finals and faced Houston in a tough seven-game series that became a defensive battle; neither team scored more than 100 points in any of the games. In the end, the defensive-minded Knicks came up short, and Houston was the champion.

While New York was awesome on defense, offensive woes continued to plague the team. For the second straight year the Knicks faced the Indiana Pacers in the semifinals. Starks and Ewing had been stellar all season. Anthony Mason, an immensely strong 6-foot-7 forward, emerged as a top sixth man, averaging 9.9 points and 8.4 rebounds per game, shooting .566 from the field. But in the seventh game of the Indiana series, Ewing missed a layup that would have tied the game, and the Knicks went home. Riley took the loss hard and stepped down as coach.

All-Star Larry Johnson.

Allan Houston, an outstanding shooting guard.

1 9 9 7

Chris Childs recorded his second career triple-double in a game versus the Charlotte Hornets.

The next year, led by NBA veteran Don Nelson, the Knicks struggled to play .500 ball. In March, assistant coach Jeff Van Gundy replaced Nelson, and the team responded with a 13–9 run to finish the regular season. Mason shined again, and proved to be one of the hardest workers in the NBA, playing a league-high 42.2 minutes per game. He led the Knicks in assists and finished second to Ewing in points and rebounds. But the Knicks faced déjà vu in the playoffs: Michael Jordan was back in Chicago and the Bulls, winners of 72 games in the regular season, easily defeated New York in the playoffs.

Free agency changed the look of the club for the 1996–97 season. The Knicks still featured Starks, Oakley, and Ewing, but Starks was converted to a sixth man and Oakley and Ewing were aging. Mason was traded to Charlotte for All-Star forward Larry Johnson and new on the team were free-agent shooting guard Allan Houston, point guard Chris Childs, and NBA veteran Buck Williams. Charlie Ward and rookie John Wallace added youth to the mix, as the Knicks managed a 57–25 season and met Charlotte and former teammate Mason in the first round of the playoffs. The Knicks stormed past the Hornets, but after a close series in the semifinals that featured several player ejections, the Knicks were eliminated by their old coach, Pat Riley, and the Miami Heat. Still, the good mix of young players and veterans created an optimism in New York—and a prediction of another Knicks championship just around the corner.